Advanced ESL

ENGLISH DISCUSSION TOPICS

*Engaging Activities to Develop Opinions,
Critical Thinking and Debating Skills*

Nigel Openshaw

www.nigelmopenshaw.com

Contents

Dedication

To the incredible and inspiring students I had in South Korea—your dedication, hard work, and support helped shape me into the teacher I am today.

You became more than just students; you felt like family, and words alone cannot capture my gratitude.

I am deeply thankful for the unforgettable memories and lessons Korea gave me, and I will always carry them with me.

Introduction

Engaging discussion activities designed to build confidence, fluency, and natural conversation skills for intermediate to advanced ESL learners!

Great discussions happen when language feels natural—like a conversation between friends rather than a classroom exercise. This book is designed to help students build confidence in expressing their thoughts, developing opinions, and engaging in meaningful discussions on real-world topics.

These lessons adapt to different class structures and timing needs with flexible, reusable activities. Whether you're working with teens or adults, the goal remains the same: to create a space where students can easily explore ideas, challenge perspectives, and speak.

This isn't about memorizing perfect sentences—it's about using English effortlessly, authentically, and engagingly.

Let's start the conversation.

Lesson 1.

Using Adjectives Effectively

This lesson promotes using adjectives correctly while describing a well-known subject.

OBJECTIVES:

Use multiple adjectives while describing something to supply a better explanation.

Describe a subject in relevant situations.

THINGS TO DO:

Choose a topic from the Resources section.

Create a practice worksheet or a short task if students are unfamiliar with adjective order.

A simple adjective order is available in the Resources section. However, specific ordering may vary.

LESSON PLAN

1. WARM-UP:

Introduce the primary lesson theme selected in the To Do section.

Explain the correct placement of adjectives before a noun.

Mention the end aim to use adjectives to describe an object further.

2. LEARN:

Write the six definitions from the Resources on the board and discuss them.

Make sure that students understand the meaning of each word.

Ask the students to supply adjectives for each term and place them in quotation marks.

Introduce the adjectives from the To Do section if students have not already done so.

Ask students to create categories, such as size, and brainstorm more terms to fit each type.

Create a table using the provided categories and display three examples on the board.

Discuss the order of adjectives when they come before a noun.

Ask students to construct a phrase with a noun and three adjectives.

Pick an object from the classroom, like a clock.

Describe it using a variety of adjectives while keeping its name a secret.

Challenge the students to identify the object being described by scanning the room.

Ask other students for additional adjectives to keep the activity going.

3. INSTRUCT:

Ask students to follow the example provided and write descriptions for selected items.

Pair or group students and ask them to find an item and provide three adjectives to describe it.

Repeat the process until everyone understands the procedure.

4. EXERCISE:

Encourage students to be creative and describe anything they see, even out the windows, and if it is visible to everyone.

The students will be limited to five guesses; if the class cannot guess the answer, the student will win.

Continue playing until everyone has had a turn or there are no more items.

5. ASSESS:

Ask follow-up questions after repeated sentences to assess student understanding.

Describe the primary topic and categories addressed.

If there is time, explain a few other uncommon objects, such as a door hinge.

BONUS - CLASSROOM WORD KNOCKOUT:

Write a noun on the board and randomly select two or three students.

Give them 20 seconds to construct a sentence quietly while standing before the class.

After a minute, ask the students for their sentences; the first grammatically correct sentence is the winner.

Repeat the process with new students until everyone has had a turn, then play champion of champions with only the winners.

RESOURCES

ADJECTIVES ORDER:

Quantity: To discuss amounts and numbers, explore terms such as "two," "many," and "several."

Opinion: Use descriptive words like "lovely," "amazing," and "delicious" to express your opinion about a topic.

Size: Enhance vocabulary with adjectives such as "tall," "big," and "short" to describe the size of an object or person.

Physical quality: Develop descriptive language by using words like "thin," "fat," and "slim" to talk about physical appearance.

Shape: Describe the form of an object with words like "square," "round," and "triangular."

Age: Use adjectives like "young," "old," and "15-year-old" to discuss a person or object's age.

Colour/Color: Add colour/color to language by using descriptive terms such as "pink," "purple," and "flame red."

Material: Use words like "wooden," "metal," and "plastic" to describe the fabric of an object.

Origin: Learn to discuss the source of something using adjectives like "Japanese," "Swedish," and "American."

Purpose: Discuss the function or intent of an object using words like "cooking," "sewing," and "cleaning."

BANKING - FINANCE TERMS:

Withdraw, Account, Statement, Bankrupt, Borrow, Exchange

Cash, Credit Card, Currency, Debt, Deposit, Rate

Loan, Mortgage, Invest, Pay, Save, Savings

Investment, Cashier, Check, Shares, Customer, Budget

CITY - URBAN SHOPPING:

Street, Avenue, Square, Building, Street Light, Pavement/Sidewalk

Road, Fountain, Park, Bus Stop, Crossing, Bridge

Bargain, Cheap, Cost, Expensive, Instalments/Installments, Price

Purchase, Receipt, Wallet, Discount, Refund, Spend

EVENTS - SPECIAL OCCASIONS:

Fancy Dress, Christening, Family Gathering, Wedding, Get Together, Anniversary

Birthday, Fireworks, Barbecue, Social, Funeral, Dinner

Bonfire, Holiday, Religion, Memorial, Display, Festival

Halloween, New Year, Procession, Valentine's Day, Christmas, Graduation

ENVIRONMENT: NATURE AND ISSUES

Nuclear Energy, Solar Energy, Conservation, Nuclear Waste, Forest Fires, Global Warming

Greenhouse Effect, Nuclear Power, Ozone Layer, Pesticide, Pollution, Waste

Wildlife, Oil Slicks, Exhaust Fumes, Aerosol, Acid Rain, Unleaded Petrol

Rain Forest, Protected Animal, Climate, Animal Welfare, Protesters, Endangered

FOOD - CONTAINER TYPES:

Bottle, Can, Carton, Bag, Bowl, Cone

Dish, Envelope, Folder, Tube, Jar, Jug

Case, Crate, Drawer, Hamper, Tub, Bucket

Basin, Basket, Bin, Box, Cabinet, Backpack

FOOD - COOKING AND EQUIPMENT:

Bake, Boil, Broil, Fry, Grill, Poach

Roast, Scramble, Simmer, Steam, Braise, Stew

Can Opener, Fork, Strainer, Spoon, Spatula, Knife

Rolling Pin, Ladle, Microwave, Mixing Bowl, Paper Towels, Timer

HOBBIES - CAMPING AND EQUIPMENT:

Adventure, Fishing, Night, Day, Forest, Sleeping Bag

Sunscreen, Boots, Cabin, Camp Fire, Wildlife, Map

Flashlight, Compass, Backpack, Tent, Bottle, Hunting

Insects, Nature, Park, Path, Trip, Insect Repellent

MEDIA - INSTRUMENTS AND SINGING:

Composer, Tempo, Lyrics, Melody, Musician, Notes

Opera, Rhythm, Singer, Song, Instrument, Tenor

Cymbal, Clarinet, Drum, Flute, Guitar, Harmonica

Piano, Saxophone, Trombone, Trumpet, Violin, Xylophone

MEDIA - MOVIE GENRES AND ROLES:

Actor, Actress, Characters, Critic, Director, Hero

Action, Adventure, Animation, Documentary, Drama, Foreign

Review, Script, Plot, Producer, Hero, Villain

Horror, Musical, Romance, Sci-Fi, Fantasy, Thriller

MEDIA - THE ARTS AND PERFORMANCE:

Audience, Backing Group, Cast, Composer, Conductor, Drummer

Guitarist, Musician, Orchestra, Pianist, Producer, Singer

Carving, Drawing, Painting, Pottery, Sewing, Ballet

Concert, Exhibition, Film, Play, Opera, Sculpture

NATIONALITIES - WORLD COUNTRIES:

Argentinian, Greek, Austrian, Belgian, Brazilian, Canadian

Chinese, Danish, Finnish, French, German, Australian

Indian, Israeli, Japanese, Mexican, Filipino, Russian

Singaporean, Korean, Spanish, Swedish, British, American

PERSONAL - EMOTIONS AND FEELINGS:

Admiration, Calm, Caring, Excited, Generous, Glad

Happy, Kind, Love, Crazy, Afraid, Frightened

Gloomy, Lazy, Lonely, Anger, Anxiety, Boredom

Cruel, Embarrassed, Envious, Naughty, Greedy, Exhausted

PERSONAL - MEMORY AND THE MIND:

Brain, Emotion, Genius, Idea, Intellect, Knowledge

Analyse/Analyze, Calculate, Forget, Memorise/ Memorize, Identify, Remember

Logic, Memory, Mind, Skill, Talent, Opinion

Work Out, Brainy, Bright, Gifted, Imaginative, Intelligent

SCIENCE - COMPUTER BASICS:

Help, Drawing, Games, Folder, Internet, Network

Open, Save, Delete, File, Spreadsheet, Document

Output, Input, Keyboard, Mouse, Printer, Scanner

Software, Memory, Monitor, Database, Interactive, Hardware

SCIENCE - SPACE AND INSTRUMENTS:

Planet, Space, Craft, Station, Suit, Weightlessness

Astronaut, Earth, Gravity, Launch, Moon, Orbit

Computer, Satellite, Microchip, Microscope, Microwave, Technician

Speedometer, Thermometer, Inventor, Researcher, Scientist, Robot

SPORTS - ATHLETIC EQUIPMENT:

Football, Basketball, Bowling Ball, Baseball, Mask, Saddle

Helmet, Skates, Sports Shoes, Pad, Outfit, Shuttlecock

Bike, Racing Car, Bat, Cue, Golf Club, Golf Ball

Flag, Skis, Surfboard, Racket, Hockey Stick, Target

SPORTS - PHYSICAL ACTIVITIES:

Car Racing, Paragliding, Snowboarding, Gymnastics, Horse Racing, Motorcycle Racing

Cycling, Skiing, Golf, Squash, Table Tennis, Tennis

Baseball, Basketball, Bowling, Football, Handball, Hockey

Polo, Rugby, Soccer, Volleyball, Athletics, Swimming

TRAVEL - ADVENTURE ACTIVITIES:

Airport, Check-In, Fly, Land, Landing, Plane

Take Off, Destination, Journey, Passenger, Travel, Baggage

Camp, Cruise, Excursion, Hostel, Hotel, Luggage

Motel, Tourism, Suitcase, Tour, Tourist, Vacation

12

Lesson 2.

Fact vs. Opinion Debating

This lesson introduces debating. Students will discuss a claim and examine solid reasons for and against it.

OBJECTIVES:

Understand the meaning of a statement and find arguments.

Express one's viewpoint and prepare an effective response to a claim.

THINGS TO DO:

Select a topic from the resources provided.

Prepare three arguments for and against the chosen claim for further comprehension.

LESSON PLAN

1. WARM-UP:

First, explain to the students how to construct arguments and present their viewpoints during a debate.

Introduce the selected topic from the To Do section.

Discuss the primary lesson goal for students to evaluate arguments for and against a specific issue.

2. LEARN:

Write the topic on the board and discuss it with the class.

Ensure that all students understand words related to the topic.

Clarify with facts and opinions. Try with examples.

Create a table on the board with columns for "Fact" and "Opinion."

Reminding them what the difference is between them might help.

After gathering comments from the students, discuss them.

Ask the students to justify their responses to differentiate their opinions from the facts.

3. INSTRUCT:

Divide the class into groups of three to four and create a for and against section.

Write the claim and a table with headings for "Pros" and "Cons" on the board.

Distribute the A4 paper and ask the students to split it into "Pros" and "Cons" columns.

Instead of the original topic, students will write their arguments and counterarguments about the statement on the board.

After some time, they should discuss good responses and drop bad ones.

Monitor the student's progress and offer suggestions when necessary.

4. EXERCISE:

Each group should present its significant points to the class.

Note their arguments on the board.

Once each group has finished, have the class review and debate each argument.

Encourage students to weigh the merits of the facts, opinions, and pros and cons.

Allow both sides to discuss and refute each other's ideas.

The conclusion of the discussion will determine whether the argument stays, moves to the other column, or gets removed.

5. ASSESS:

Ask the students if the arguments are in the correct column.

Request that students make changes and point out inaccuracies to evaluate their comprehension.

Discuss the terms for review.

BONUS – ENGLISH COURT DEBATE:

Students are encouraged to voice their perspectives.

Place various topic cards in a box, such as "Should mobile phones be prohibited in classrooms?"

Select three students to oversee and be the judges.

Divide the remaining students into two teams: advocate for the topic and argue against it.

Select a team spokesperson to lead the discussion.

Have one team make a statement and write it on the board.

The opposing team will respond to the statement, and both sides will continue to supply fresh reasons.

After some time, the judges will decide which team presented the most compelling case.

Remember: suggest that students use respectful language, focus on the arguments rather than the people making them, and listen carefully to each other's points.

RESOURCES

ART AND CULTURE:

Art is a form of expression.

Diverse cultures have different art forms.

People use art to spread important messages.

Art and culture bring people together.

EDUCATION AND LEARNING:

Education is essential for personal and societal growth.

Different people have different learning styles.

Learning happens outside of traditional classroom settings.

Education helps us better understand the world.

ENTERTAINMENT AND MEDIA:

Entertainment and media influence our opinions and beliefs.

Different people enjoy diverse types of entertainment.

People use the media to spread positive messages.

We should be critical of the media we consume.

FAMILY AND RELATIONSHIPS:

Family is an important support system.

Respectful communication is vital in all relationships.

Families come in all shapes and sizes.

Each family has its unique dynamic.

FOOD AND COOKING:

Cooking from scratch is healthier than processed food.

Diverse cultures have unique cuisines.

Carefully reading recipes leads to better results.

Sharing meals with others brings people together.

HEALTH AND WELLNESS:

Mental health is as important as physical health.

Eating a balanced diet is vital for good health.

Sleep is essential for both physical and psychological health.

Hygiene practices prevent the spread of illness.

HOLIDAYS AND FESTIVALS:

Diverse cultures celebrate different holidays.

Holidays bring people together.

Festivals highlight various art forms and cultures.

We must respect and honour/honor other traditions.

GREETINGS AND INTRODUCTIONS:

Eye contact is essential when greeting someone.

Diverse cultures have diverse ways of greeting.

Body language communicates a greeting or disrespect.

Be polite and make an excellent first impression.

NATURE AND THE ENVIRONMENT:

The environment needs to be protected.

Climate change is a global issue.

Different human actions have different environmental impacts.

We need to work together to protect the environment.

POLITICS AND CURRENT EVENTS:

We must stay informed about current events.

Different people have different political views.

Politics affects people's daily lives.

It is crucial to engage in civil and respectful political discourse.

SCIENCE AND TECHNOLOGY:

Science and technology have improved our lives greatly.

Science helps us better understand the world.

Different scientific discoveries have other impacts.

We must use technology responsibly.

SHOPPING AND MONEY:

Budgeting helps save money.

Ethical shopping helps the environment and people.

Comparing prices enables you to make better purchasing decisions.

Credit cards are helpful or harmful, depending on their use.

SOCIAL ISSUES AND DIVERSITY:

We must respect and celebrate diversity.

Different people face different social issues.

It is vital to be an ally to those with social problems.

We should work together to create an equal society.

SPORTS AND PHYSICAL ACTIVITIES:

Exercise is essential for good health.

Different sports have different physical demands.

Playing team sports improves communication skills.

Physical activity improves our mental health.

TECHNOLOGY AND SOCIAL MEDIA:

Technology connects us from all over the world.

People use social media to spread positive words.

Social media has adverse effects on health.

We must use technology responsibly.

TRAVEL AND SIGHTSEEING:

Travelling/Traveling broadens our perspective.

Researching the destination makes the trip better.

Sightseeing is educational and fun.

Respectful behaviour/behavior when visiting other countries is essential.

TRANSPORTATION AND DIRECTIONS:

Public transportation is better for the environment.

Following directions carefully is vital for safety.

Different countries drive on different sides of the road.

Maps and GPS help you navigate unfamiliar areas.

WEATHER AND CLIMATE:

Climate change affects the whole planet.

Extreme weather events are dangerous.

Human activity contributes to climate change.

We should take steps to reduce our carbon footprint.

WORLD HISTORY AND GEOGRAPHY:

Understanding history helps us avoid making the same mistakes.

Geography affects cultures and ways of life.

Diverse cultures have different histories.

Exploring other parts of the world broadens our understanding.

WORK AND JOBS:

Different jobs have other requirements and benefits.

Education and experience help you get a job.

Challenging work and dedication lead to career advancement.

Work-life balance is vital for overall well-being.

Lesson 3.

Using Informal Phrases

This lesson tests students' creative language use. Students look for the literal meaning, but this does not result in comprehension.

OBJECTIVES:

Understand the meaning of proverbs and clichés.

Use proverbs and clichés in context to demonstrate understanding.

THINGS TO DO:

Select a subject from the Resources section.

Next, add six words related to assessing understanding.

Students will need internet connectivity to complete the task.

LESSON PLAN

1. WARM-UP:

Introduce students to proverbs and clichés using everyday language to describe a situation.

Discuss the primary lesson theme and aim: to create text using proverbs and clichés.

2. LEARN:

Provide students with the first half of a proverb and check whether they know the complete statement. For example, "A penny saved...".

Explain to students that they should express themselves even if they make mistakes.

Pose questions to gauge comprehension and invite suggestions for the next step.

Go through each word to ensure that students understand the meaning of the informal term before explaining the entire saying.

Verify that each student understands the term's meaning and clarify it for those who may be unclear.

Ask students to express their proverb interpretation in two to three phrases.

Review and edit their work to correct any mistakes.

3. INSTRUCT:

Ask the class to respond and post their responses on the board for everyone to see.

Find any students who may want to revise their definitions and then write the proper interpretation on the board.

Have students compare their definitions to the accurate description and provide examples of when to use the term.

Ask students to work in pairs or groups to produce three uses for the proverb and present their findings to the class.

4. EXERCISE:

Check on their activities to ensure they are all engaged.

5. ASSESS:

Ask each group about their prepared responses and write them on the board to prove whether students know the expression's context-specific use.

Finish the task by going through the examples provided by the students.

BONUS - EXPLORING THE ORIGINS:

As an added exercise, students research an expression's history to better understand its literal and metaphorical interpretations.

Their efforts may only be simple, but it is an excellent way to get students to collaborate freely. They will need to conduct their research on the Internet.

RESOURCES

ANIMAL-RELATED CLICHÉS:

"Do not count your chickens before they hatch"; we should avoid assuming success before it happens.

"The elephant in the room" is an obvious problem no one wants to discuss.

"A fish out of water" means someone in an unfamiliar or uncomfortable situation.

"A wolf in sheep's clothing" means someone who pretends to be harmless but is dangerous.

BUSINESS-RELATED CLICHÉS:

"Thinking outside the box" means creatively approaching a problem.

"Cutting corners" means taking shortcuts or compromising quality to save time or money.

"Moving the goalposts" means changing the rules or expectations in the middle of something.

"Putting all your eggs in one basket" means risking everything on one plan or idea.

FOOD-RELATED CLICHÉS:

"A piece of cake" means something easy to do.

"Bite off more than you can chew" means to take on more than you can manage.

"The icing on the cake" means a bonus or something that makes a good situation even better.

"Too many cooks spoil the broth" means that when too many people try to do the same thing, they may mess it up.

GENERAL LIFE-RELATED CLICHÉS:

"When life gives you lemons, make lemonade" means to turn a tricky situation into something positive.

"All that glitters is not gold" means that what looks good on the outside may not be as good as it seems.

"You cannot judge a book by its cover" means that you cannot decide the value of something based on appearance alone.

"The grass is greener on the other side" means that people think others' situations are practical elsewhere.

HEALTH-RELATED CLICHÉS:

"An apple a day keeps the doctor away" means eating healthy helps prevent illness.

"Laughter is the best medicine" means that laughter helps improve your mood and physical health.

"You are what you eat" means that your health and well-being depend on the food you consume.

"Prevention is better than cure" means that it is better to avoid a problem than to fix it later.

RELATIONSHIP-RELATED CLICHÉS:

"Love is blind" means that people in love overlook flaws or problems in their partner.

"Absence makes the heart grow fonder" means that being apart increases feelings of love and longing.

"Behind every great man is a great woman" means that a man's success is often due to the support of a woman.

"Breaking up is hard to do" means that ending a relationship is difficult and painful.

SPORTS-RELATED CLICHÉS:

"Practice makes perfect" means that by repeatedly doing something, you will get better at it.

"It is not whether you win or lose, it is how you play the game" means that how you conduct yourself is more important than winning.

"Hitting it out of the park" means doing something exceptionally well.

"Playing hardball" means being tough or challenging in negotiations.

TIME-RELATED CLICHÉS:

"Better late than never" means it is better to do something late than not.

"Time flies when you are having fun" means time quickly passes when you enjoy yourself.

"In the nick of time" means completed in time or at the last moment.

"Time heals all wounds" implies that time helps people recover from emotional or physical pain.

TRAVEL-RELATED CLICHÉS:

"Home is where the heart is" means that your true home is where your loved ones are.

"All roads lead to Rome" means that there are many ways to achieve the same goal.

"The world is your oyster" means you have endless possibilities in life.

"The journey is the reward" means that the experience of getting somewhere is more important than the destination itself.

WEATHER-RELATED CLICHÉS:

"Every cloud has a silver lining" means something positive is found in every situation.

"It is raining cats and dogs" means it is raining heavily.

"A storm in a teacup" means a small problem blown out of proportion.

"Under the weather" means feeling ill or unwell.

CHARACTER AND INTEGRITY PROVERBS:

"Actions speak louder than words" means that people's behaviour/behavior is more important than what they say.

"Honesty is the best policy" means that telling the truth is correct.

"You reap what you sow" means that your actions have consequences.

"Character is who you are when no one is watching" means that true character is revealed by what you do when no one is around.

HAPPINESS AND CONTENTMENT PROVERBS:

"Money cannot buy happiness" means material wealth does not guarantee happiness.

"Happiness is a state of mind" means that happiness depends on your attitude and perspective.

"Happiness is not a destination, it is a journey" means that happiness is found in the process, not only the result.

"Count your blessings" means focusing on your life's positive things.

HARD WORK AND SUCCESS PROVERBS:

"No pain, no gain" means working hard to succeed.

"If at first, you do not succeed, try again" means that perseverance is crucial to success.

"Life is a journey, not a destination" means that the experience of living is more important than specific goals.

"Success is 99% perspiration and 1% inspiration" means that challenging work is more important than talent.

HEALTH AND WELLNESS PROVERBS:

"An apple a day keeps the doctor away" means that healthy eating helps prevent illness.

"Early to bed and early to rise makes a man healthy, wealthy, and wise" means that going to bed and waking up leads to a healthy and prosperous life.

"You are what you eat" means your diet affects your health and well-being.

"Laughter is the best medicine" means that laughter and joy will improve your health.

LIFE LESSONS PROVERBS:

"Actions speak louder than words" means that people's behaviour/behavior is more important than what they say.

"It is never too late to learn" means that you learn new things, regardless of age.

"Where there is smoke, there is fire" means that if there are rumours/rumors or signs of something, it is true.

"Honesty is the best policy" means that telling the truth is correct.

MONEY AND WEALTH PROVERBS:

"Money does not grow on trees" means that money is not easy to come by.

"Time is money" means time holds value and should be used effectively.

"A penny saved is a penny earned" means that saving money is the same as earning money.

"Money cannot buy happiness" means material wealth does not guarantee happiness.

RELATIONSHIP PROVERBS:

"To have a friend, be a friend" means that you must be friendly to make friends.

"A rolling stone gathers no moss" means that people keep moving to avoid becoming stagnant.

"Birds of a feather flock together" means that people with similar interests or backgrounds tend to hang out together.

"Love conquers all" means that love is more powerful than any obstacle or problem.

TIME AND PATIENCE PROVERBS:

"Rome was not built in a day" means that good things take time and effort.

"Time heals all wounds" implies that time helps you overcome emotional pain.

"Good things come to those who wait" means patience leads to success and happiness.

"Patience is a virtue" means being patient and not rushing things, which is good.

TRUST AND LOYALTY PROVERBS:

"Trust takes years to build, seconds to break, and forever to repair" means it is hard to regain trust once it is lost.

"Actions speak louder than words" means that people's behaviour/behavior is more important than what they say.

"Honesty is the best policy" means that telling the truth is correct.

"A true friend is constantly loyal" means that real friends stick by each other through thick and thin.

WISDOM AND KNOWLEDGE PROVERBS:

"The proof of the pudding is in the eating" means that you can only judge the quality of something by experiencing it.

"The more you learn, the less you know" means that the more you know, the more you understand how much is unknown.

"A penny for your thoughts" means asking someone to share their ideas or opinions.

"You learn something new every day" means there is something to learn.

36

Lesson 4.

Moral Dilemma Challenge

Students should think about various scenarios and evaluate their own moral decisions. In each case, what would they do?

OBJECTIVES:

Encourage students to discuss morality and ethics.

Students evaluate moral dilemmas using critical thinking skills.

THINGS TO DO:

Select a problem from the Resources section.

Find two relevant tales online and create a simple reading exercise for practice.

Select six words from the moral statement and expand on each one.

LESSON PLAN

1. WARM-UP:

Introduce values and ethics and explain the lesson's aim to examine moral and ethical options in certain circumstances.

Introduce the primary lesson theme from the To Do section.

2. LEARN:

Discuss the To Do section words and ask for student opinions.

Introduce the dilemma to be explored.

3. INSTRUCT:

Provide students with a story related to the topic and ask them to consider the situation and debate whether it is good.

Compile a list of opinions from the students.

4. EXERCISE:

Discuss the situation with the class and ask for their opinions on the best action.

Encourage students to consider the perspective of the individuals in the story and reflect on whether they would make the same decision again.

It is not a decision of each other but rather an assessment of different perspectives.

5. ASSESS:

Compare the students' original ideas with the discussion at the end of the lesson.

Assess both sides of the debate and appreciate how students respond to different points of view.

Remember to make the activity enjoyable and not push any uncomfortable students.

BONUS - TWENTY QUESTIONS CHALLENGE:

Select a single student from the group.

Randomly select a word and give it to the student to keep a secret.

Other students can only ask "yes" or "no" questions and have twenty guesses to get the word right.

Once they guessed correctly, a new round with a different student would start.

RESOURCES

These resources prompt consideration and discussion of ethical issues.

ENVIRONMENTAL:

How important is it to protect the environment?

Should everyone preserve the environment?

What can you do to reduce your carbon footprint?

Is using products that harm the environment OK if they are cheap?

How do you manage a situation where someone is damaging the environment?

Should companies be held responsible for their impact on the environment?

How do you make sure you are recycling correctly?

Is it right to cut down trees for development purposes?

GENERAL DILEMMAS:

What are the pros and cons of waking up early?

Is it better to do homework first or play video games?

How do you balance chores and free time?

Should you tell the truth or lie to avoid trouble?

Is it OK to cheat in a competition to win?

How do you manage a friend who mistreats you?

What actions should you take if you witness bullying?

How do you deal with peer pressure?

HUMAN RIGHTS:

How important are human rights?

Should everyone have the right to free speech?

What should you do if someone violates someone's rights?

Is it ever OK to discriminate against someone?

What can you do to address mistreatment?

Does everyone have the right to practice their religion?

Is it right to punish someone without a fair trial?

What can you do if you see discrimination?

JUSTICE AND FAIRNESS:

Is it fair for some people to have more than others?

How can we treat all races equally?

How do you ensure that we include diversity?

What is the best way to resolve a conflict?

Should everyone have the same rights?

How do you react to unfair treatment?

Is it right to punish every criminal?

What can you do if someone mistreats another person?

LOYALTY AND BETRAYAL:

Is it ever OK to break a promise?

How do you deal with a friend who has betrayed you?

How important is loyalty in a friendship?

Is it OK to keep a secret from a friend to protect them?

How do you forgive someone who has betrayed you?

What do you do when your friends are unfriendly?

Is it wrong to gossip about your friends?

What do you do if your friend does something wrong?

PERSONAL INTEGRITY:

Is it OK to keep a secret from a friend?

How do you stand up for what you believe in?

Is it OK to copy someone else's work?

How do you respond to a request to do something wrong?

How do you admit when you are wrong?

What do you do when someone is mean to you?

Should you say sorry even if it was not your fault?

How do you forgive someone who has hurt you?

PRIVACY AND CONFIDENTIALITY:

Is it OK to read someone's diary without permission?

Should you share others' secrets if it could help them?

How do you protect your privacy?

Should parents have access to their child's phone?

Is it OK to take photos of others without their permission?

How do you deal with someone sharing your data?

Should schools be allowed to search students' lockers?

How do you handle a friend who is too nosy?

RESPONSIBILITY AND DUTY:

What are your responsibilities at home?

How do you balance school and social life?

Is it OK to procrastinate on a project?

What should you do if you forget to do something?

How do you manage a difficult task?

What can you do if you have not prepared for a test?

Helping others: when is it your responsibility?

How do you take responsibility for your actions?

TRUTHFULNESS AND HONESTY:

Is it ever OK to lie?

How to be honest without offending?

What should you do if you see someone else lying?

Keeping spare change from cashier: ethical or not?

What to do when honesty might get you in trouble?

Is it OK to tell the truth if someone else gets in trouble?

Is it wrong to tell a lie to avoid hurting someone?

How do you forgive someone who has lied to you?

TRUST AND LOYALTY:

How important is trust in a relationship?

Is it OK to break a promise for a good reason?

What should you do if someone breaks your trust?

How do you manage a situation where someone is dishonest with you?

Should you trust someone who has lied to you before?

Is it OK to tell a secret to someone who is not trustworthy?

How do you build trust with someone who does not trust you?

What do you do if your friend tells you a secret you promised to keep?

Lesson Extras

Conversation Starters

The following list includes over 250 discussion starters for various subjects.

ART:

Calligraphy, Drawing, Graphic Design, Painting, Photography, Printmaking, Sculpture, Street Art

BUSINESS:

E-commerce, Entrepreneurship, Finance, Human Resources, Innovation, Leadership, Marketing, Supply Chain Management

CULTURE:

Customs, Dance, Fashion, Festivals, Food, Heritage, Music, Traditions

DEPRESSION:

Anxiety, Chronic, Coping Strategies, Medication, Mental Health, Mindfulness, Psychology, Self-Help, Therapy

ENVIRONMENT:

Climate Change, Environmental Activism, Environmental, Policy, Green Living, Pollution, Renewable Energy, Sustainability, Wildlife Conservation

FITNESS:

Cardiovascular Training, Exercise, Meditation, Nutrition, Sports, Strength Training, Wellness, Yoga

GENDER ROLES:

Feminism, Gender Equality, Gender Stereotypes, LGBTQ+, Masculinity, Sexuality, Transgender Rights, Women's Health

HISTORY:

American History, Ancient History, Archaeology, Genealogy, Historical Figures, Historiography, Modern History, World History

INNOVATION:

AI, Bioengineering, Futurism, Inventions, Nanotechnology, Robotics, Science, Technology

JUSTICE:

Activism, Advocacy, Criminal Justice Reform, Equality, Human Rights, Judicial System, Restorative Justice, Social Justice

KNOWLEDGE:

Critical Thinking, Education, Learning, Personal Growth, Research Methods, Self-Improvement, Study Techniques, Wisdom

LOVE:

Attachment Styles, Communication Skills, Dating, Heartbreak, Intimacy, Marriage, Relationships, Romance

MOVIES:

Actors, Cinematography, Directors, Film Industry, Film Theory, Movie Genres, Reviews, Screenwriting

NATURE:

Birdwatching, Ecotourism, Environmentalism, Forest Bathing, Kayaking, National Parks, Rock Climbing, Wildlife Photography

ONLINE DATING:

Catfishing, Ghosting, Long-distance relationships, Messaging etiquette, Online safety, Profile authenticity, Swiping culture, Virtual dates

POLITICS:

Corruption, Diplomacy, Electoral systems, Humanitarianism, International relations, Lobbying, Political polarisation/polarization, Populism

QUESTIONS:

Epistemology, Ethics of artificial intelligence, Free will, Meaning of life, Metaphysics, Morality, Philosophy of science, Religion and morality

RELIGION:

Atheism, Cults, Faith, New Age spirituality, Religious art, Rituals, Sacred texts, Worship practices

SELF-EXPRESSION:

Creative non-fiction, Fiction writing, Journaling, Personal blogs, Podcasting, Poetry, Public speaking, Stand-up comedy

TRAVEL:

Adventure sports, Backpacking, Couchsurfing, Food tourism, Luxury travel, Road trips, Sustainable tourism, Volunteer travel

URBAN LIFE:

Community gardens, Food deserts, Gentrification, Public art, Smart cities, Transit-oriented development, Urban sprawl, Walkability

VIDEO GAMES:

First-person shooters, Gamification, Gaming addiction, Indie games, Role-playing games, Simulation games, Streaming culture, Virtual reality

WOMEN'S RIGHTS:

Body positivity, Gender-based violence, Intersectional feminism, Reproductive rights, Sexual harassment, Wage gap, Women in leadership, Women's health policies

XENOPHOBIA:

Anti-Asian racism, Anti-Blackness, Anti-Indigenous discrimination, Anti-Semitism, Ethnic cleansing, Hate speech, Islamophobia, Racial profiling

YOUTH CULTURE

Online activism, Social media influencers, Teenage pregnancy, Youth employment, Youth justice, Youth mental health, Youth subcultures, Youth voting

ZEITGEIST:

AI ethics, Cancel culture, Climate activism, Cryptocurrency, Digital minimalism, Memes as communication, Mental health awareness, Streaming wars

There Is More!

*Embark on an exciting learning journey
with our Intermediate ESL English
Discussion Topics book!*

This book is the first of two to help enhance English language proficiency and build discussion confidence.

The other book features engaging modules that cover an array of topics, such as:

Expanding Speaking Keywords - Discover new ways to articulate ideas and augment the vocabulary.

Conversation Starter Strategies - Sharpen conversational skills and ask and answer questions efficiently.

Communication with Synonyms - Broaden language capabilities by exploring unfamiliar words and phrases.

Follow-Up Conversational Skills - Cultivate the ability to participate in deep and meaningful conversations.

Everyday Casual Conversations - Learn how to use colloquial language and slang in various social situations appropriately.

Do not miss taking English to the next level! Order a copy of the Intermediate ESL book today.

52

Positive Classroom Environment

As a teacher, remember that your success may be measured partly by your students' grades and pass rates.

So, while academic achievement is essential, we must prioritize building a positive classroom environment. Meeting the needs and interests of our students requires flexibility and adaptability.

Keep in Control

Students will respond well to a confident and competent teacher, so it's vital to set yourself up as the class leader. If you feel overwhelmed, take a moment to regroup and make any necessary adjustments to your approach.

One helpful tip is to practice remembering your students' names and paying attention to what they say in class. This will go a long way toward building rapport and creating a positive learning environment.

To stay prepared, consider making notes at the end of each lesson and reviewing them before the next class.

We must help students who may have missed an earlier lesson or are struggling to keep up. Consider setting up an after-class meeting or offering more resources and support. Proactively responding to students' needs helps ensure their success.

Thank Your Students

I am grateful to the outstanding and motivational students I enjoyed teaching in South Korea. They provided me with the foundational training and experience that helped me grow as a teacher and better understand my students' unique needs.

While I aimed to adhere to standard guidelines and best practices in the classroom, my students pushed me to focus more on meeting their needs, so I adapted my teaching.

In addition, their eagerness to learn and enthusiasm for education inspired me to be a better teacher and continually seek new ways to help them succeed.

I hope you can say the same about your students.

Best wishes on your teaching journey!

Growth Beyond the Classroom

Improvement does not stop when one leaves the classroom. Adjusting to a new culture and language can be challenging, especially for foreign English teachers.

Respect and collaborate with local teachers and students and be open to different learning needs and abilities. "Your perception of what it means to be a teacher may differ from that of local teachers. They want you to be like their model of a foreigner before your teacher's opinion. Do not rock the boat; you are a guest in their country.

Improve Personal Performance

To make progress, find and address barriers, even for non-routine tasks. Seek input from others and consider a different approach. When brainstorming, it can be helpful to write down all options and keep an open mind. Anticipating issues reduces uncertainty, so improving one's confidence is crucial.

Identify areas for improvement and take action to make progress. Change poses challenges, but seeing the need for change is crucial. Reflect on current situations to decide on improvement and seek help. Remember, seeking help is a step toward progress, not a sign of weakness.

Communicate Better Options

To build positive relationships and foster trust, we need to seek help from others. We must also take the time to care for them and show interest in their lives. When communicating with others, we must appreciate their perspective.

Experience Joy and Positivity

Enjoying teaching is essential for a teacher. If it becomes a chore, look for places of gratitude and ways to push beyond what is needed. Maintain a positive attitude in any circumstance and pay attention to emotions. Reflection is vital for personal growth and progress, so assess past experiences to learn and improve.

Enjoying the journey toward our goals reduces stress and creates positive memories.

Good luck. Hard work pays off in the end.

Let's Share the Love!

Thank you so much for reading!

As a self-published author, every reader means the world to me. Your support keeps me creating, sharing, and growing.

I'd love to hear your thoughts on whether you found value in this book. A short review at the store where you bought it helps others discover my work—and makes a huge difference.

Your words matter more than you know. Thank you for being part of this journey with me!

With gratitude,

Nigel

About the Author

I create from experience, from what I've lived, learned, and felt. This isn't just a book; it's a piece of my journey, shared with you.

I'm Nigel—a lifelong learner, creator, and explorer of ideas. My journey has taken me from teaching ESL in South Korea to backpacking across Australia and New Zealand and now to a quieter, more creative life. I believe in the power of curiosity, small intentional actions, and creating work that sparks inspiration and growth.

My books reflect the things I care about most:

* Writing and storytelling—I create resources that inspire, engage, and help others learn, from travel memoirs to ESL activity books.

* Mental Health & Well-being—I draw from personal experience and research to explore mindfulness, burnout, and self-discovery in my writing.

* Gardening & Sustainable Living – With over 30 years of growing wisdom, I share insights on kitchen gardening, inspired by my grandfather's love for the earth.

* Art & Creative Expression—I create every book cover and illustration. I believe visuals should feel as connected to the story as the words.

Beyond books, I'm always experimenting—whether exploring numerology, diving into gaming, or capturing the beauty of nature through photography. Everything I create is about connection, growth, and seeing the world differently.

— Just a lonely layabout, left to my own devices—that's me. I strongly believe in lifelong learning for personal growth. Therefore, I am always eager to discover new interests and expand my horizons. I bring this passion to my writing.

I have even created a free app called Numerology Colors that offers insights into one's numbers based on their name and date of birth. It is an entertaining and informative way to explore numerology and better understand oneself.

If you want to learn more about my projects, please visit my website at www.nigelmopenshaw.com